How to Draw Zen Doodle Animals

Meditating with a Zen doodle Menagerie

By Veronica Kim

Contents

What you will find here:

Introduction

Welcome to the art of Zendoodle animals. In this book you are going to discover that you can create Zendoodle art through drawing animals and that through these drawings you are going to find a place to relax and focus within yourself.

Each drawing has been carefully chosen to not only maximize your potential but also to show you that you can do these drawings. The animals within will help you focus as you draw them and as you watch them come to life on the paper before you your confidence will increase. And what's more, you are going to realize that you are the one bringing them to life even as the act of drawing brings a new level of relaxation and focus to your own thoughts.

Remember, this is not a task, this is a pleasure. Do not become frustrated with what you are doing because that will simply defeat the purpose of Zendoodle art. Take each page that you are going to draw upon and understand that the page is blank and that you are going to be creating something upon it. You are not forced to do this, you are choosing to do this. You are taking a step forward to calm your mind, to slow down your life, to see the beauty in the world, and to see the beauty that you can create with Zendoodle animals.

Disclaimer

While all attempts have been made to verify the information provided in this book, the author doesn't assume any responsibility for errors, omissions, or contrary interpretations of the subject matter contained within. **The information provided in this book is for educational and entertainment purposes only. The reader is responsible for his or her own actions and the author does not accept any responsibilities for any liabilities or damages, real or perceived, resulting from the use of this information.**

The trademarks that are used are without any consent, and the publication of the trademark is without permission or backing by the trademark owner. All trademarks and brands within this book are for clarifying purposes only and are the owned by the owners themselves, not affiliated with this document.

What you will find here:

Zendoodle art is a beautiful, carefree form of abstract art that has been used by many people to relax and free their minds in order to meditate.

Zendoodle method has spread from the small studio of Maria and Rick to the entire world. Zendoodle art can literally be found on display in galleries in Massachusetts and all the way to galleries in Tokyo. People have discovered not only an inner peace while working upon their own Zendoodle images but that they have an innate ability to create art as well.

The use of Zendoodle art to draw animals will help people to focus their thoughts and to realize not only their own potential to create art but also to understand and realize how truly relaxing and healing the practice of Zendoodle art can be. Here in these pages the new Zendoodle artist will find several things:

- How to draw Zendoodle animals

- Discover that Zendoodle art is not difficult

- Understand that Zendoodle art frees the mind

- Learn to relax and focus while drawing

- Discover that they too can create beautiful art

Introduction

Welcome to the art of Zendoodle animals. In this book you are going to discover that you can create Zendoodle art through drawing animals and that through these drawings you are going to find a place to relax and focus within yourself.

Each drawing has been carefully chosen to not only maximize your potential but also to show you that you can do these drawings. The animals within will help you focus as you draw them and as you watch them come to life on the paper before you your confidence will increase. And what's more, you are going to realize that you are the one bringing them to life even as the act of drawing brings a new level of relaxation and focus to your own thoughts.

Remember, this is not a task, this is a pleasure. Do not become frustrated with what you are doing because that will simply defeat the purpose of Zendoodle art. Take each page that you are going to draw upon and understand that the page is blank and that you are going to be creating something upon it. You are not forced to do this, you are choosing to do this. You are taking a step forward to calm your mind, to slow down your life, to see the beauty in the world, and to see the beauty that you can create with Zendoodle animals.

Chapter – 1

The Zen doodle Dolphin

Perhaps no other animal in the sea brings up images of both happiness and joy than the dolphin. It is a playful animal often seen following ships or swimming alongside of them. When the dolphin disappears beneath the waves it is a reminder of how free and unburdened their lives are. Drawing a Zen dolphin, then, is an act which should be a freeing experience, a way to let go of your worries and your problems as you watch the image slowly come to life before your eyes.

All Zendoodle art begins with a small piece of white paper, a square which is roughly three and a half inches by three and a half inches. The drawings are done with ink and there are no mistakes in Zendoodle art. Everything becomes incorporated. That being said, however, this is your first experience with Zendoodle art and we do not want you to feel that this would be too stressful for you as you begin your journey in to Zendoodle method.

Instead of beginning with ink and a small piece of paper, please feel free to use a larger piece of paper and a pencil. Just remember, though, that this is a way for you to relax and forget about your worries. Do not bring your concerns and issues to the art.

So, let's start with a normal sized piece of paper and a pencil because it's time to begin.

1. Take your pencil and starting just off center of the sheet draw a slight arc moving from left to right, stopping at about the halfway point if you were to draw a full arc.

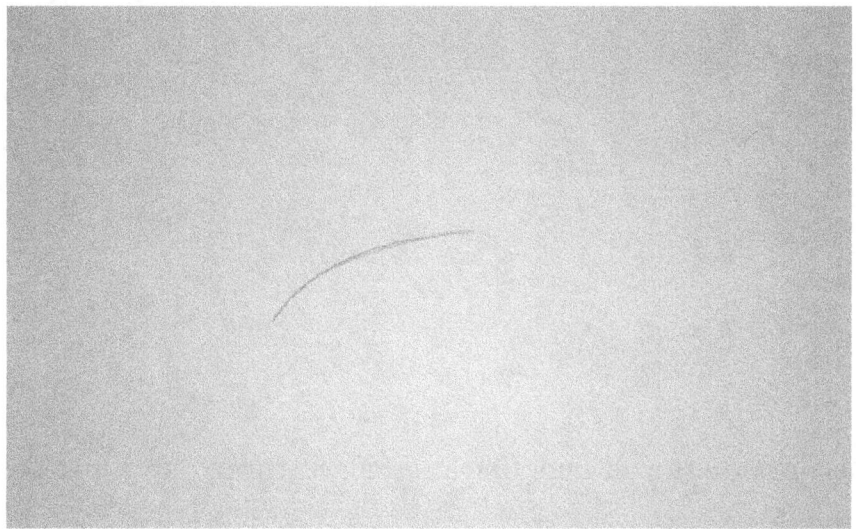

2. At the top of your arc you are going to bring a new line up at a higher angle to the right, creating a nearly straight line about an inch long. From the top of your new line you are going to make another small line, perhaps a quarter of an inch long, moving sharply to the right. And then, from that line, you are going to bring a line down that slightly curves in so that its end is in line with the end of your initial arc.

3. From here you may find it easier to turn your paper so that the point you have drawn in step 2 is facing to your right. Once you have done that place your pencil at the end of your last line and draw a gentle curve as if you were completing the initial arc that you had started in step one.

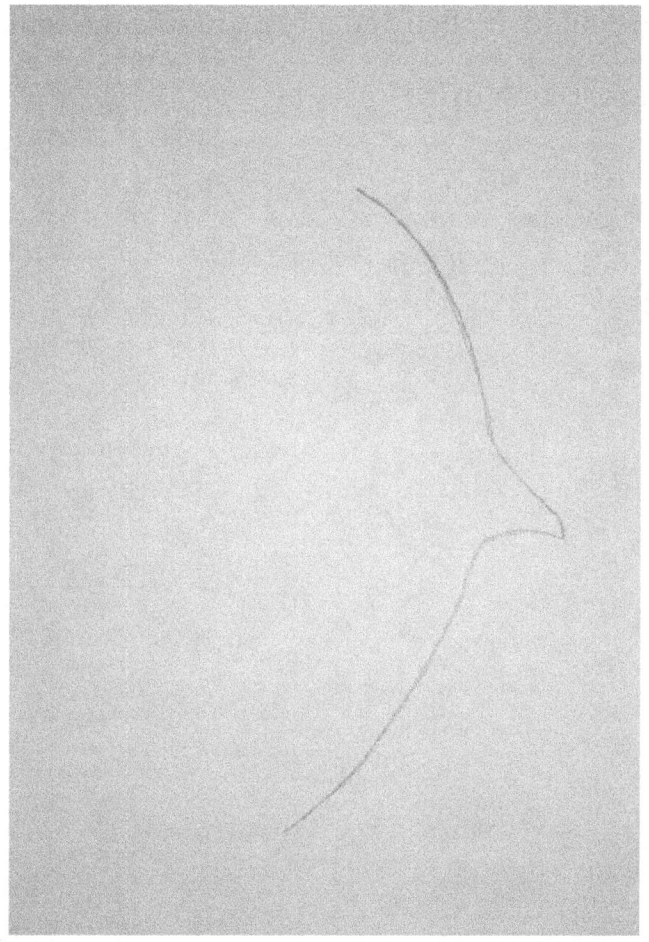

4. Rotating the paper clockwise, so that the point is facing towards you, place your pencil on the start of your first line and draw a short, one inch line out to the right at a slight, upwards angle. When you reach the one inch mark draw a small arc curving back in towards the center of the page, creating a backwards 'C' shape. When you finish with the top of the backwards 'C' bring the new

line out to an inch and a half towards the center with a slight dip in the center of it.

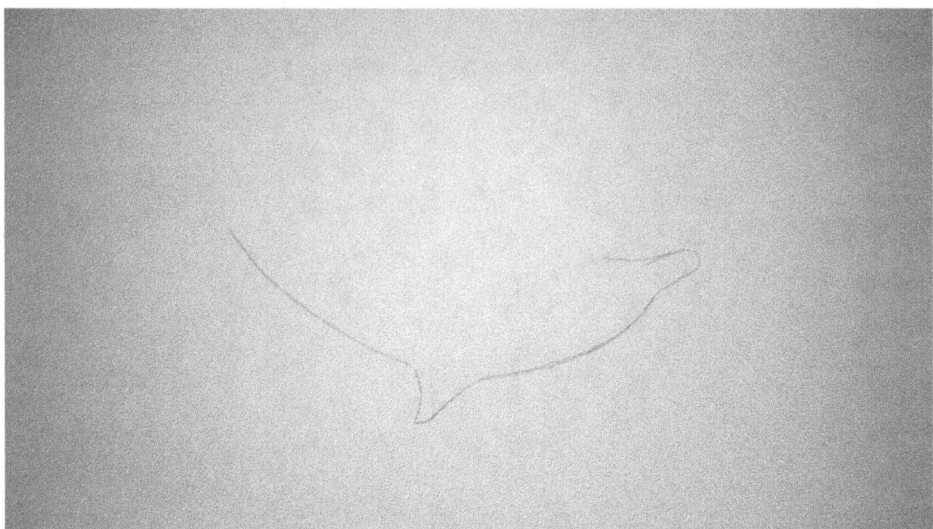

5. For the next step you can turn the paper so that the fin faces to the right once more. From the last point you drew you bring out another line, with a low arch towards the upper fin. When you finish this arc draw another soft arc out to the left of page angling down. After an inch gently curl the line back in straight towards the body you are creating and stop parallel to where the line began.

6. Placing your pencil at a quarter of an inch down the flipper's straight line, draw a gently curves to the left and that runs parallel to the dolphin's back. Once you bring that line to stop roughly across from the end of the dolphin's back, you begin to draw the tail. For the tail you draw a pair of lines. The first line curves from the bottom of the body in a half moon shape with the crest of the curve facing towards the top left of the page. The

second line curves down from the top of the body with the crest of its curve facing the bottom right corner of the page. Then, to finish the tail, you connect the two lines by drawing a reverse "C" which faces in towards the body and the upper right corner of the page.

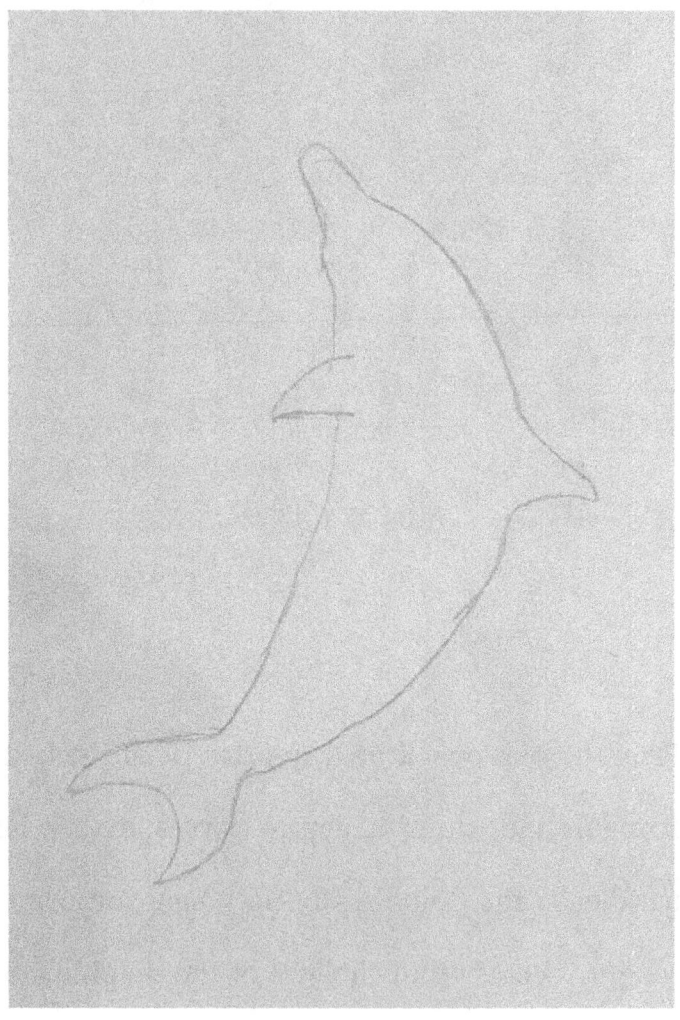

7. Turning the page so that the dolphin once more looks proper you may take your ink and ink in the lines, giving them a sharper definition than you had obtained with your pencil. Then, once you have finished the lines and gotten comfortable with your pen, you draw a small, dark eye just behind the top of the dolphin's nose.

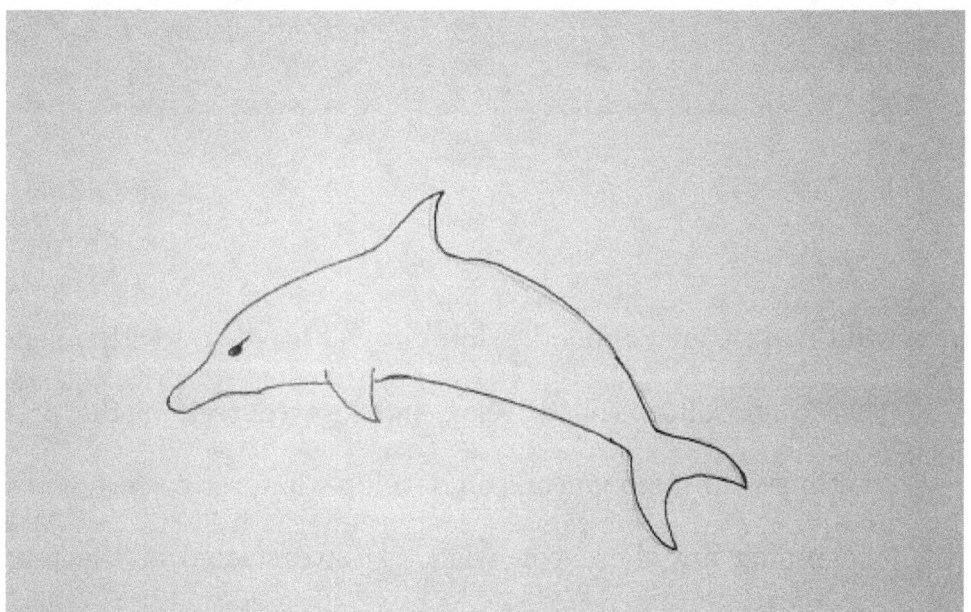

8. Finally, you draw the dolphin's mouth, a softly arching line from just above the beginning of the snout to nearly an inch back towards the body. With this done you can begin fill in your Zendoodle Dolphin!

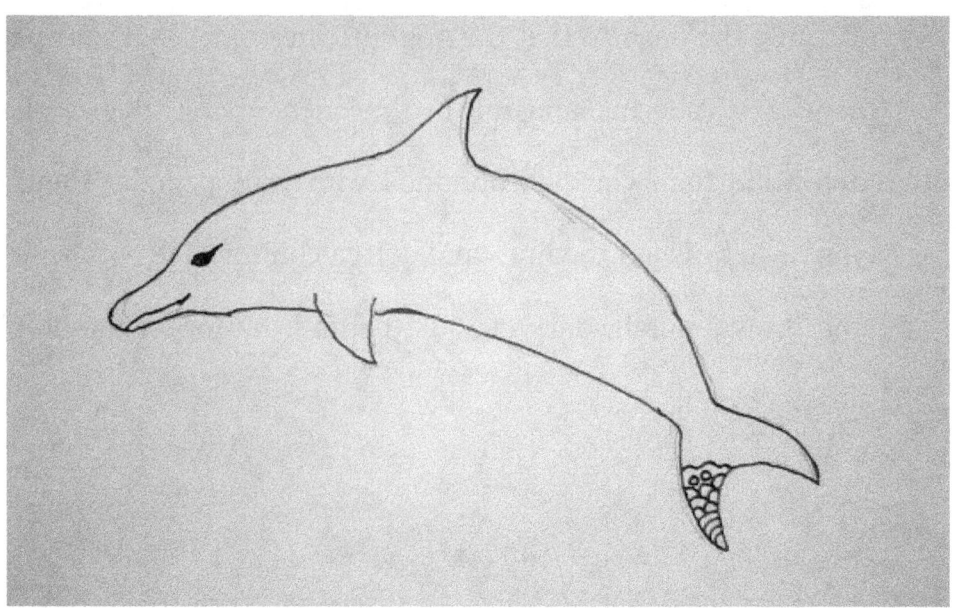

9. Filling in your Zendoodle dolphin will leave you with a sense of peace and allow you to relax and lose yourself in the process. Letting your mind go you can develop whatever pattern you wish, beginning anywhere you wish. I have started at the tail and slowly worked my way forward, letting the lines move themselves through the dolphin's body until my inner self tells me that the work is done.

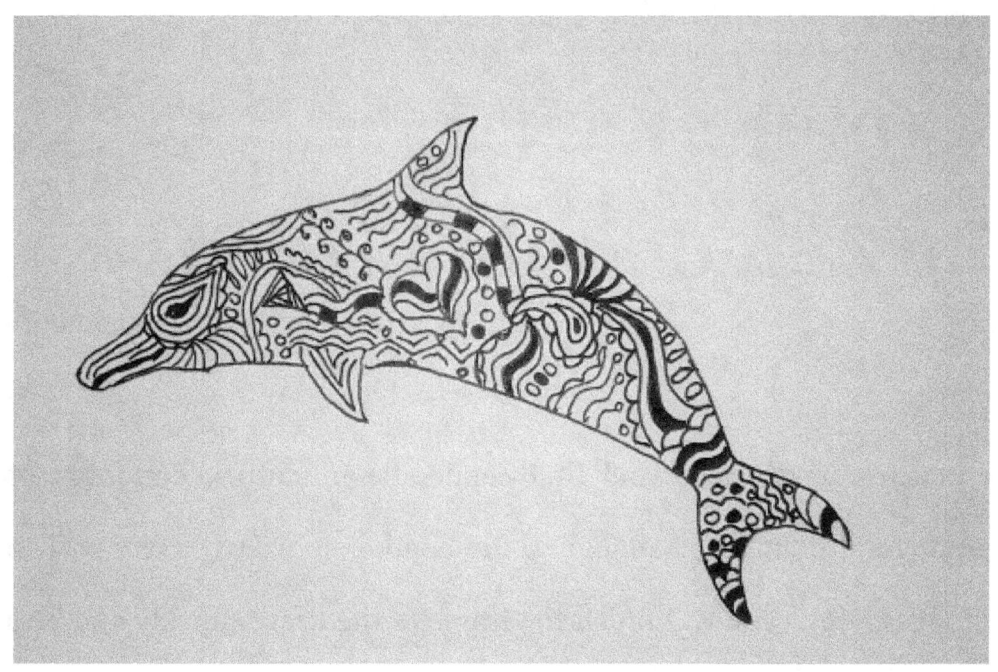

Congratulations!

You have just finished your first Zendoodle piece of art! By following these simple steps you have brought a dolphin to life on a page where there was nothing before. As you drew this dolphin and allowed your inner self to populate the empty space within the dolphin you were creating a place of peace and relaxation. Now that you have finished your dolphin, it's time to move on to the Zendoodle Lizard.

Chapter 2:
The Zen doodle Lizard

Now that you have drawn your first Zendoodle animal you can move on to something a little more challenging, the Zendoodle lizard. Here we'll start with longer lines. You will finish the frame of the lizard quickly and be able to devote more time to the Zendoodle art which you will bring forth within the lizard itself.

1. Starting once more with a blank page and your pencil start at the left hand side of your page and start drawing an inverted "J", with the hook facing to the left and the curve reaching towards the top of the page. Bring the straight line of the inverted "J" down to just below the halfway point of the page. Then, starting at the hook, draw a curving line the follows the initial line on the inside, slowly widening as you move towards the first lines end. Just as you reach the point where the curve ends, start to really widen the second line, curving it out to the left of the page so that when you finish the line

it ends just about an inch under the end of the first line and facing towards the right hand side of the page.

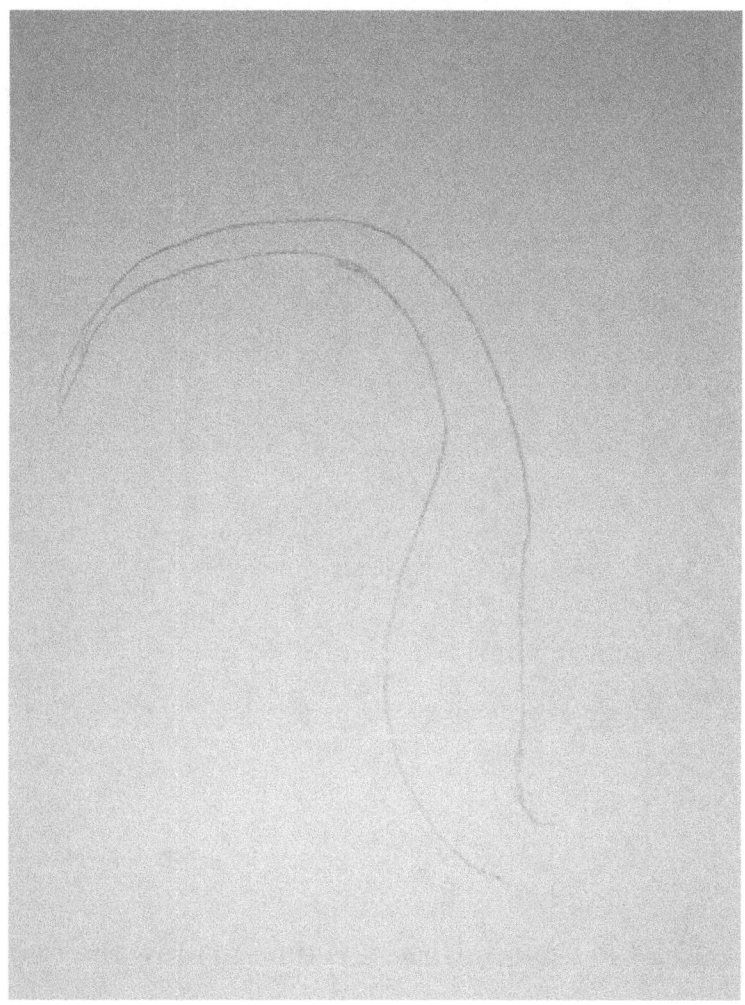

2. With this done turn the page counter-clockwise so that the tail of your lizard is facing to the left and now you can begin to draw the lizards head. From the top line curve slightly out to the left and

then bring the line back towards the upper right. Then, from the bottom line draw a line with a slight arc to connect with the upper line.

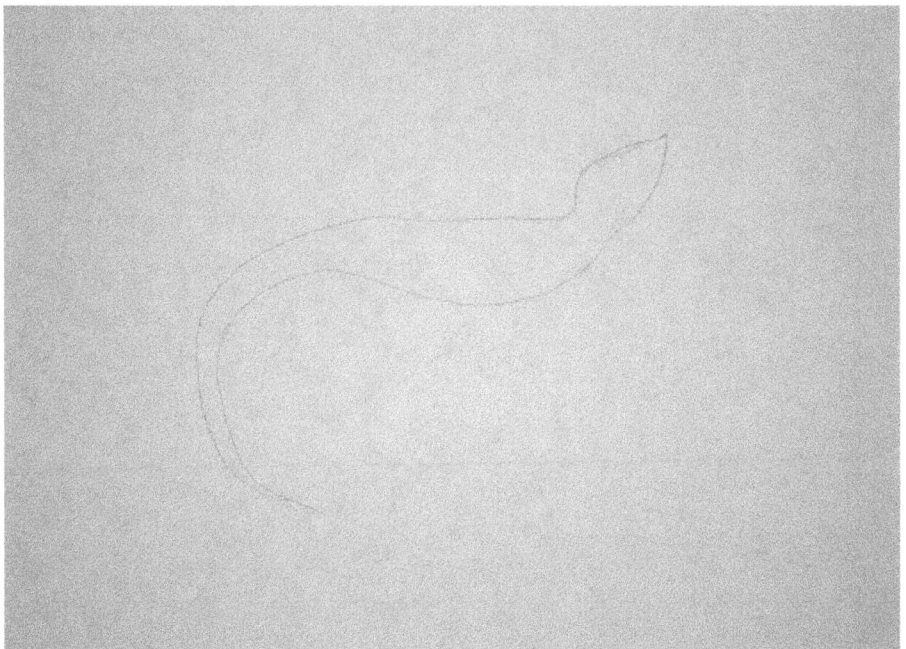

3. With the head finished it is time to draw the four legs. Turn the page so that the head of the lizard is now facing straight up. The first leg on the left will have only three toes and will start about half an inch below the head. The line will curve first down then up, with the toes being evenly placed from right to left, and as the last toe is finished draw a fresh line arcing in to a point nearly a quarter of an inch from the body. From there you bring the line

back up to the body in another slight arc. The next three legs are drawn in roughly the same fashion, with four toes instead of three. Remember to keep the lines smooth and flowing, nothing rigid or harsh.

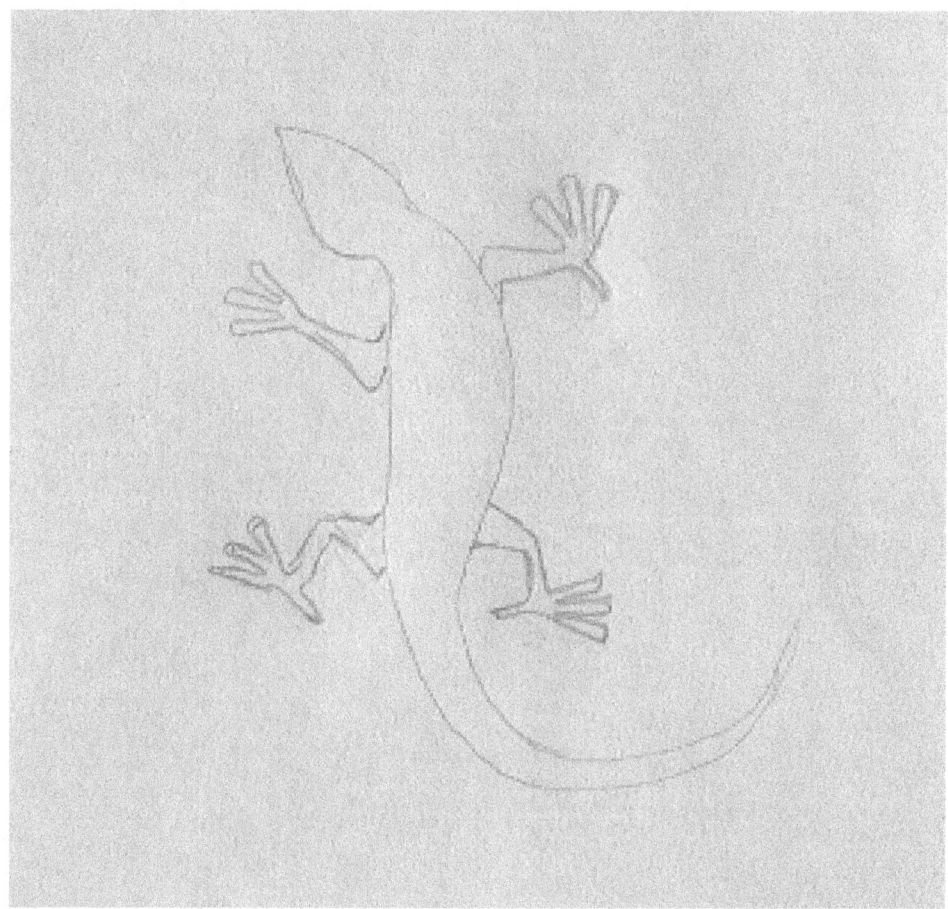

4. Once you have finished the legs, making sure that they are spread apart and evenly placed, it's time to draw the eyes. The eyes are simple, two small round dots atop the lizard's head placed a short

distance apart and as if they represented the 2 and 7 positions on a dial clock. Make sure that the eyes are colored in and dark.

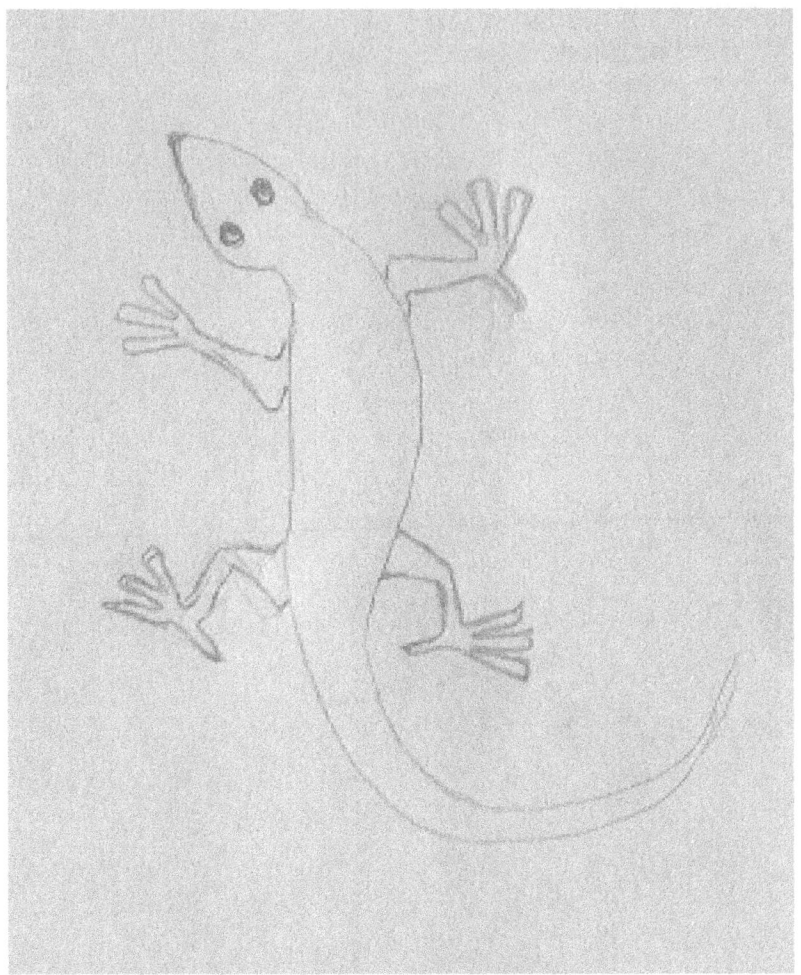

5. Now that you have finished the pencil work of your lizard, turn the page once more so that the lizard's head is facing to the right. When this is done take out your pen and begin to ink in the lines, giving them the amount of definition that you want to see. You

can either fill in the eyes completely or if you choose only fill them in partway, making it seem as if the lizard is looking at something. When inking, however, make sure that you follow the line of the legs down and up from the body's line. Do not connect the body lines and then ink the legs since that will ruin the fluidity of your lizard.

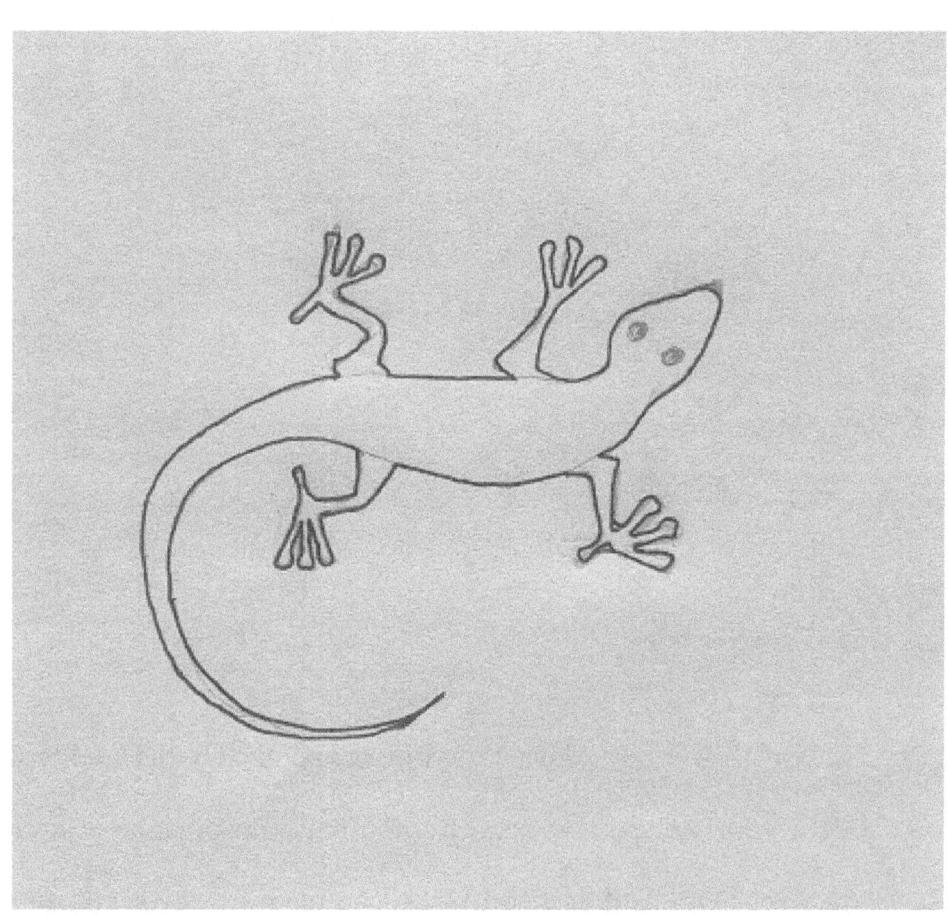

6. Your next step, if you choose, would be too take an artist's eraser and carefully work away the pencil lines left behind by your pencil work.

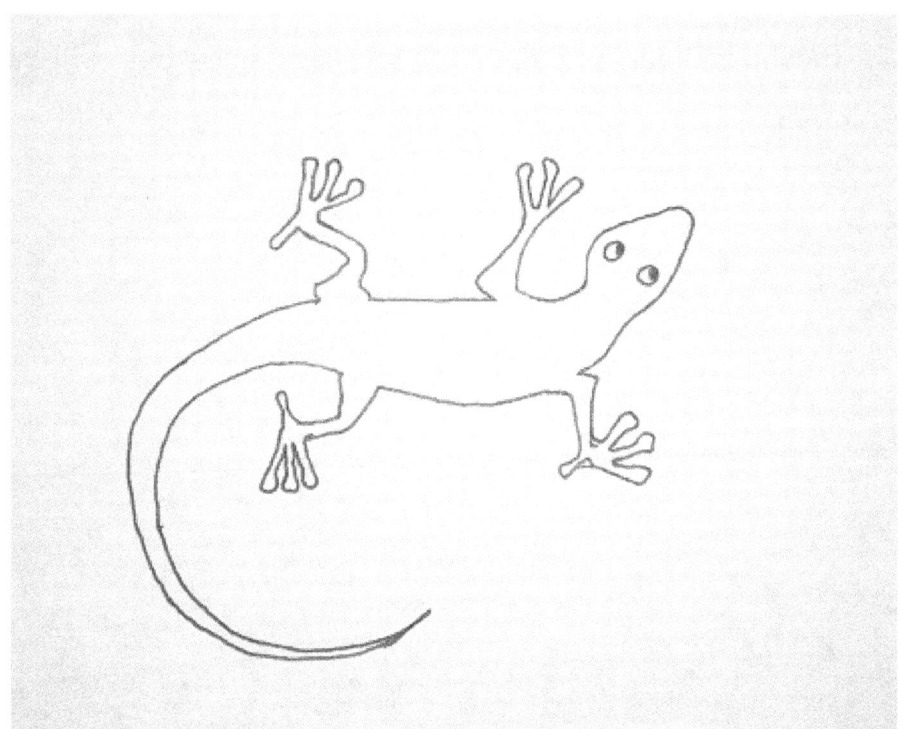

7. Now, with the boundaries of your lizard clearly defined, you can begin your Zendoodle art. Remember, the designs you choose are your own, and you can move the page however you need to. Again, do not feel a need to follow any specific pattern. Make your own, or, even better, let your inner self choose the design to make within the lizard you have drawn.

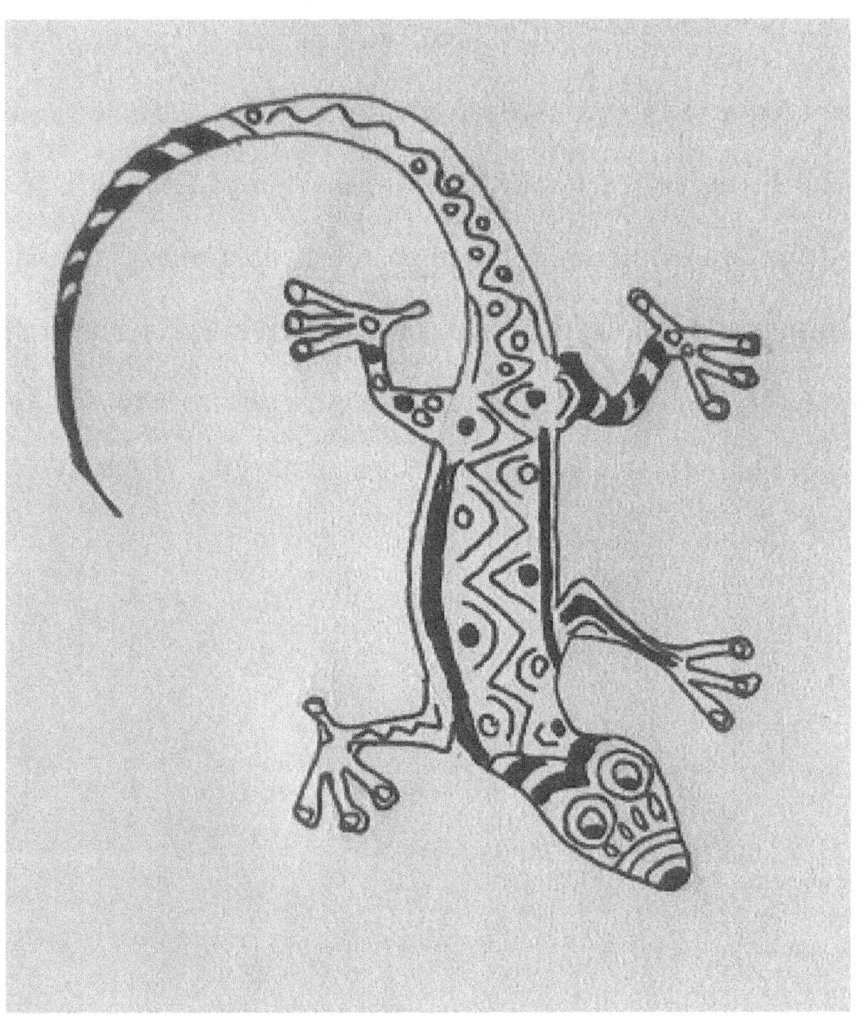

Well done! The Zendoodle Lizard was definitely more difficult than the dolphin, requiring you to think as you formed the legs and toes of the lizard. The lizard was also a far different space for you to work within as you created the Zendoodle art. The finished lizard, however, should remind you each time that you look at it that you have created a beautiful piece of art, and that you had a powerful sense of calm and inner restfulness as you let the images flow from your pen.

Chapter 3:
Zen doodle Shapes

Shapes are the basic foundations for any drawing and in Zendoodle art the shapes can serve not only as foundations but as art in and of themselves. Whether you place the shapes together on a page and work with them, or if you place one shape upon a page by itself, you can create beautiful works of art with the most basic of shapes.

In the following photographs you will see a trio of shapes placed on the same page. These photographs are, of course, only a suggestion, a guide post, if you will, towards a wide range of Zendoodle art.

1. Taking up your pencil and a clean sheet of paper you can begin by drawing three shapes upon the page, leaving however much room between each shape as you choose. Let's start with a square, a triangle, and a circle.

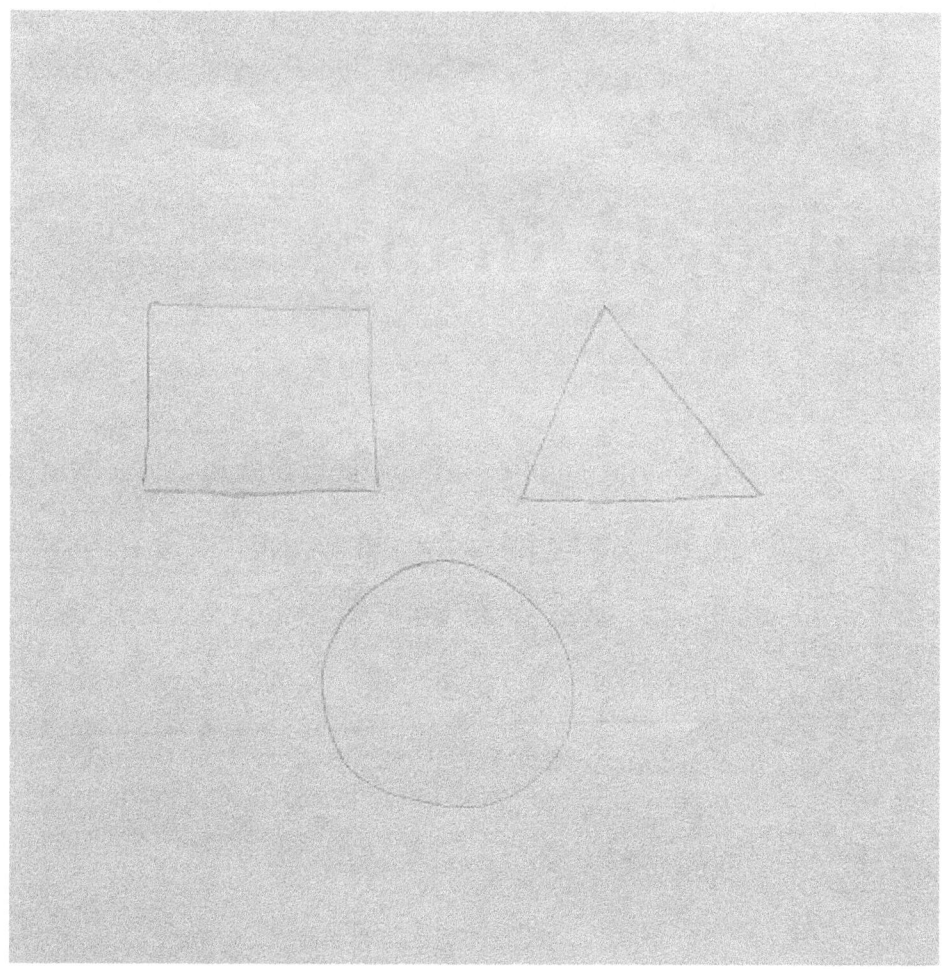

2. Once you have drawn your three shapes, remembering to draw loosely and naturally, you can put your pencil aside and take your pen up once more. With a steady hand trace the lines of the shapes so that they stand out brilliantly, ready for the next step.

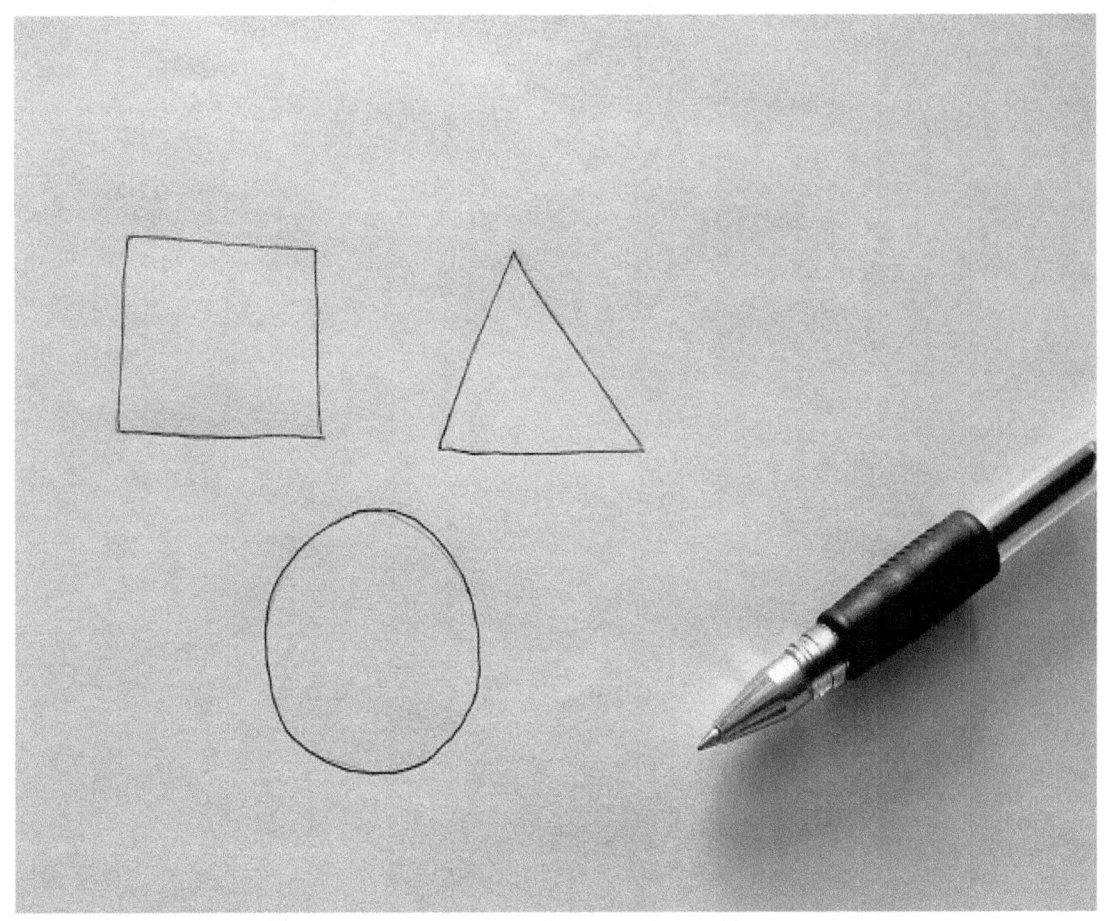

3. The next step, of course, is to begin creating your Zendoodle art within the confines of the shapes. Each shape will lend itself to a wide array of Zendoodle art, an art which is only inhibited by your own imagination.

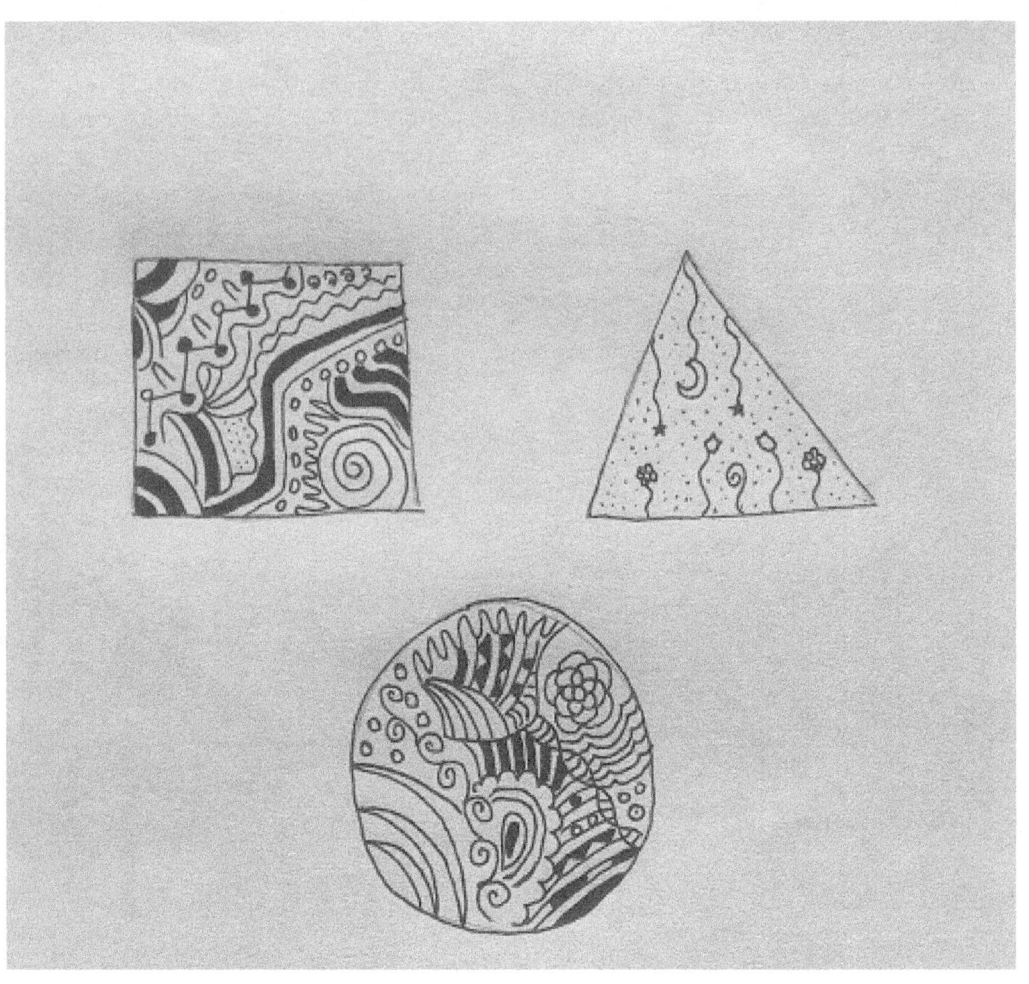

4. Once you have finished your Zendoodle art within the shapes you can try something new. If you have colored pencils or fine-point markers of different colors you can start to color in the shapes. Let your inner self choose the various colors and watch as the shapes slowly come alive under your hand.

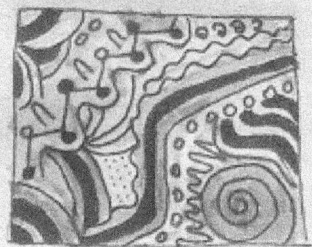
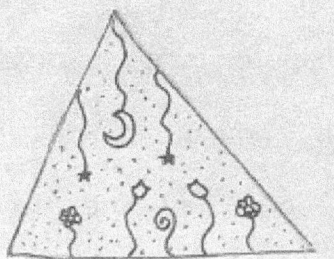
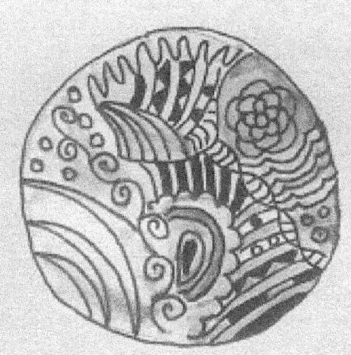

Since you mastered the Zendoodle dolphin and lizard the shapes were next to allow you relax a little more and to show you that you could master the simple shapes as well. There is no need for you to be concerned about a specific shape or image. You are fully capable of completing any object placed before you and of being able to transform that object into a stunning image of Zendoodle beauty. These simple geometric shapes, filled with a physical representation of your own inner peace, will be beautiful gifts to people who need a reminder that while life is complicated they can slow it down and find peace within themselves through Zendoodle art.

Chapter 4:
A Zen doodle Pigeon

Birds are a joy. And even the pigeon, which seems to inhabit every city in the world, is a beautiful sight. It is completely natural, then, for us to seek to draw something as plain, yet as beautiful, as a pigeon. And since the pigeon itself does not seem bound to any sort of structured life, so too should you create Zendoodle art within the boundaries of a drawn pigeon.

1. Once more take up your pencil, making sure that it is sharp and ready, and place your paper in front of you. In the center of the page start with a "J" shape, beginning with the end of the hook. As you reach the top of the straight line start to curve the line up and out to the right. When the line has gone roughly an inch and a half over towards the right, and down about an inch, flare the line out to the right just a little.

2. Starting at the end of the "J"'s hook, bring the line up so that it's even with the curve at the top of the "J" from step one. Once you have reached that point gently bring the line out and to the left, angling slightly for three to four inches. Then, beneath the end of the "J"'s hook, leaving perhaps an inch between them, start a new line and angle it down, curving gently to the left for three to four inches as well.

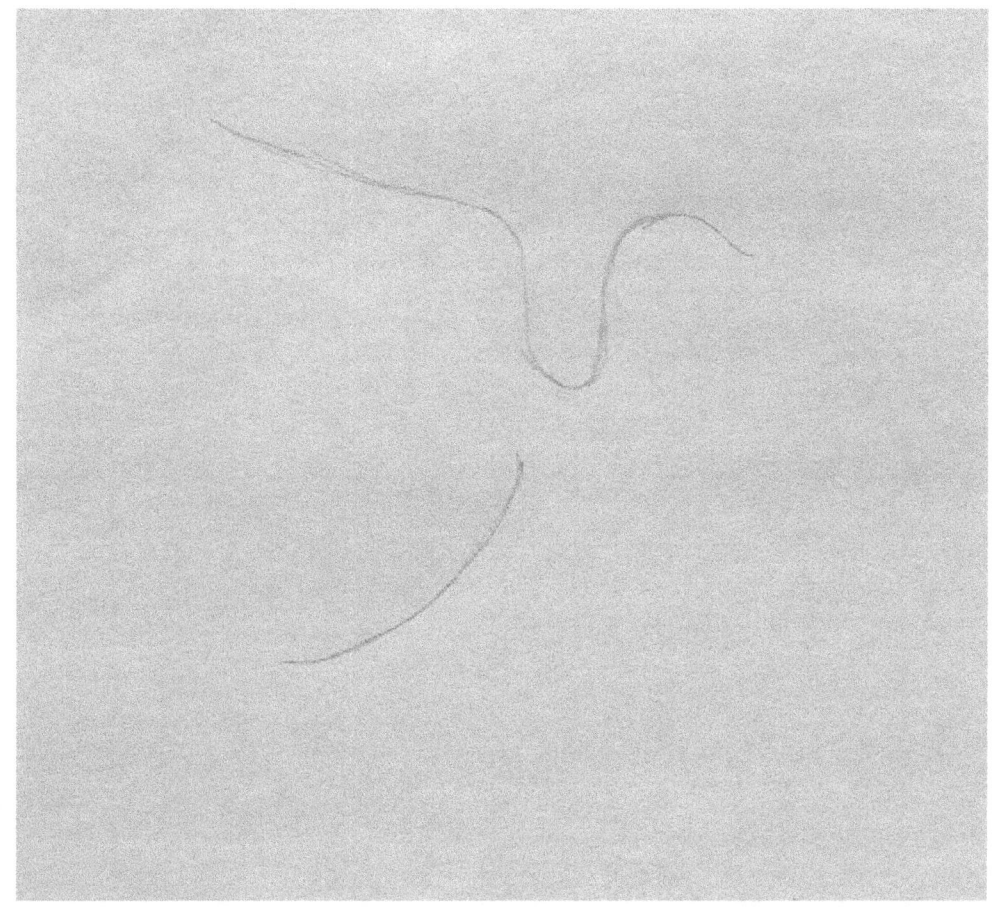

3. Your next step will be to bring the pigeon's left wing to life. You can do this by connecting the two left lines together. Starting at the top left line begin connecting the two lines by making five partial arcs, each arc lower than the previous and moving down to connect with the lower line. When this is done you will have a wing that looks as though it's waiting for you to supply the definition to the wings.

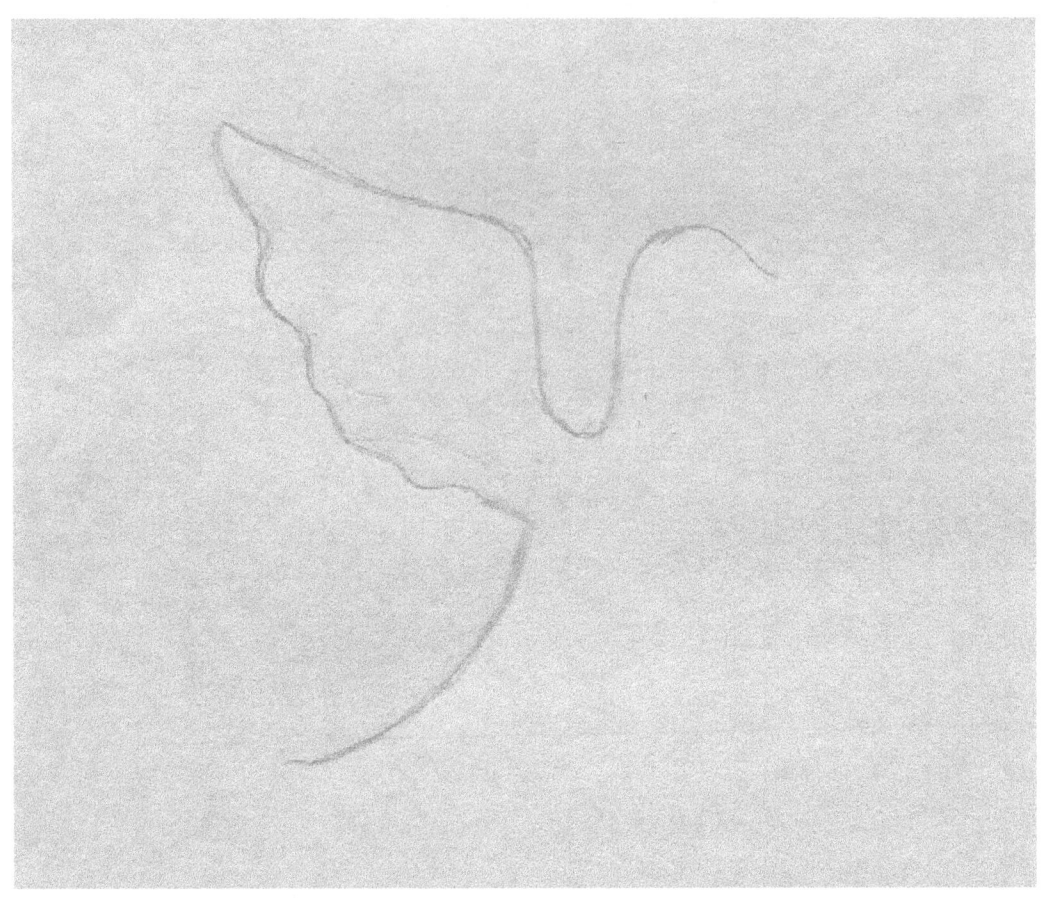

4. Starting at the flare to the right which you made in step one it's time to define the beak and the breast of the pigeon. After placing your pencil at the end of the flare, bring a new line in slightly back to the left at a downward angle. Once you have done that for roughly a quarter of an inch begin to curve back out to the right and at a slightly descending angle. Bring this curve out to form the pigeon's breast. Once you have curved the line down to where it would be in line with the juncture of the wing

line and the downward flare of the tail feathers, start to bring the line back up, stopping roughly at the halfway point of the tail feathers and leaving an inch between the end of your new line and the tail feathers. Then, from that point, draw a line that angles ever so slightly to the left for about two inches. After you have completed this line you can now connect this line to the end of the tail feathers. As you do this you can make a series of small arcs to give a rough definition to the tail feathers themselves.

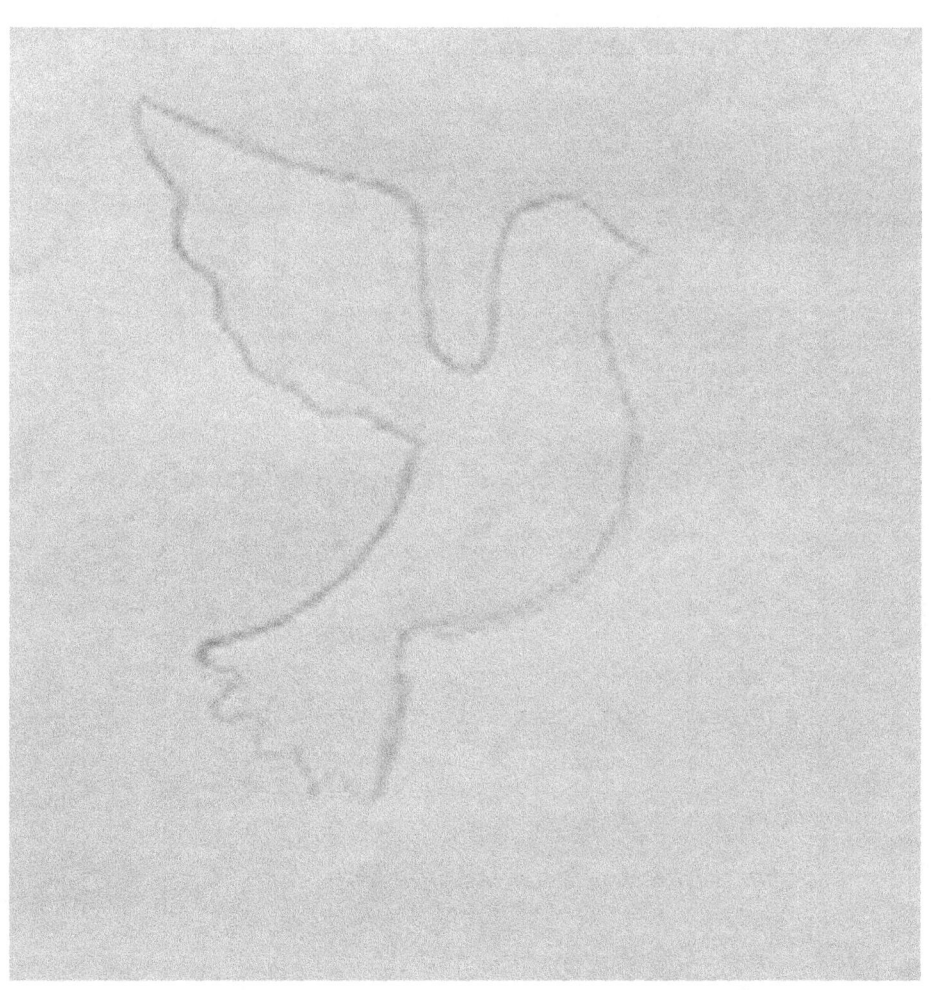

5. Now that you have finished the main body of the pigeon you can go back up to the pigeon's head. From there, starting at the left and just half an inch in from the left of the head's beginning, bring a line up straight for a moment before curving it slightly to the right and up. Once you have gone about two inches create a point and then bring the line in a slight outward arc down to the pigeon's beak, connecting the line to the pigeon's head just about an eighth of an inch from the end of the beak.

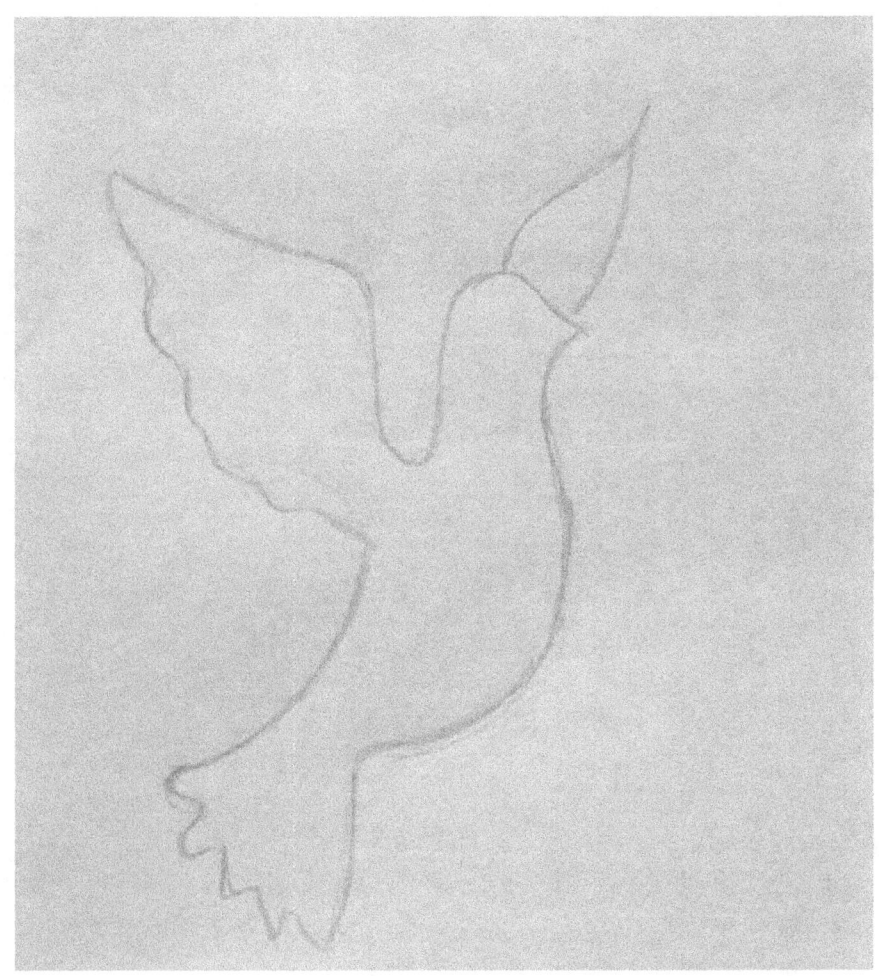

6. The next step is to draw the pigeon's eye, just a small circle placed a short distance behind the beak and below the pigeon's brow.

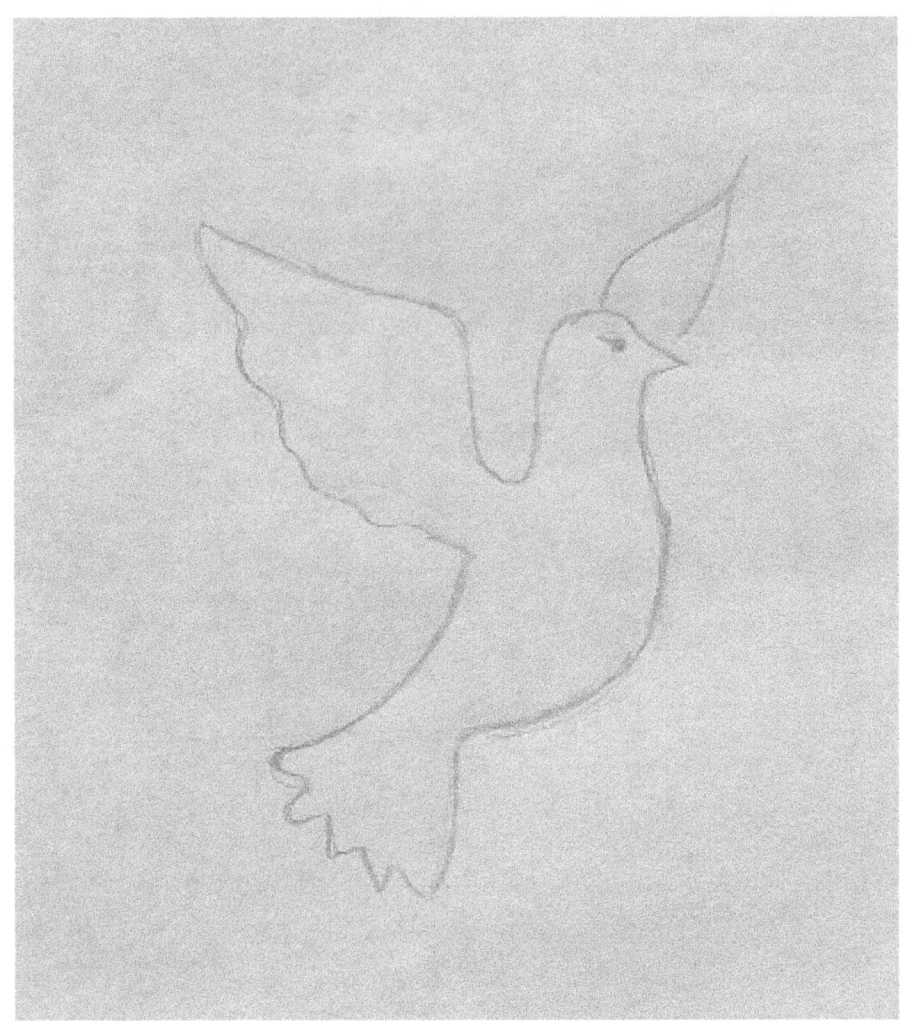

7. Now that you have completed the rough, pencil outline of your pigeon, you can put your pencil down and take up your pen. Using your pen carefully go over the lines of your pigeon, preparing it for the Zendoodle art which you are about to create.

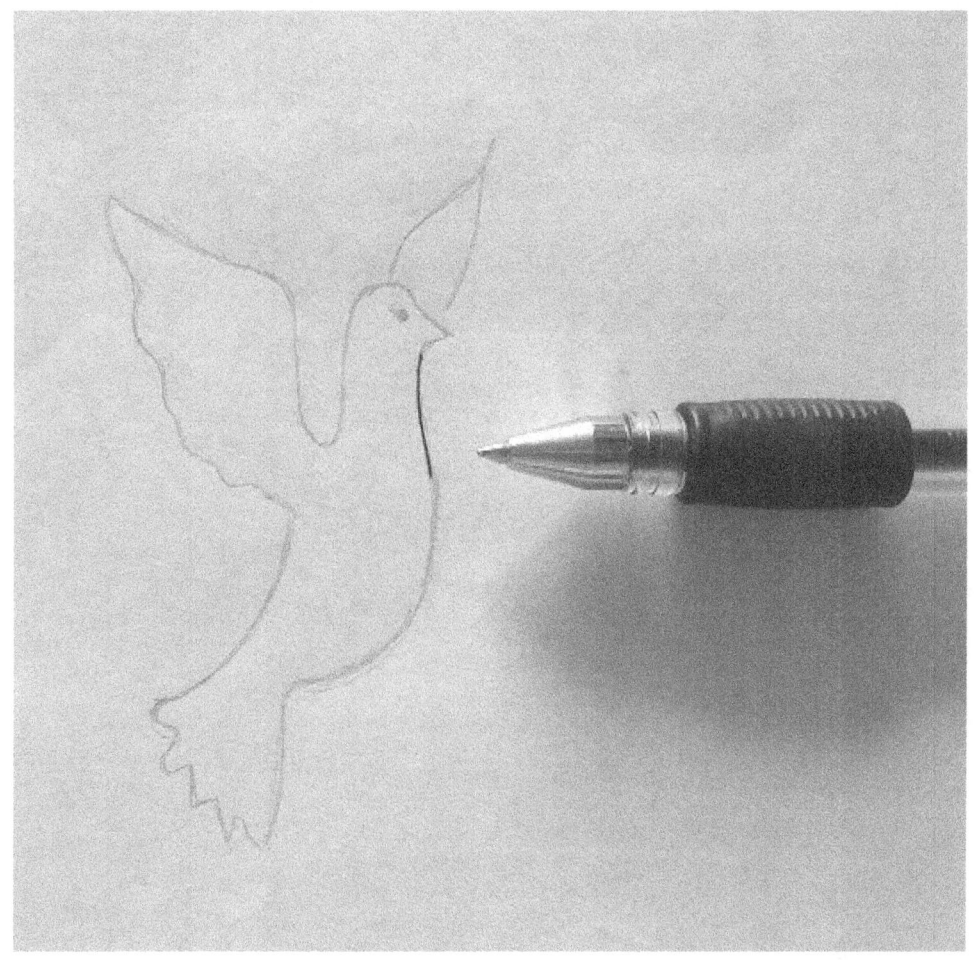

8. Once you have finished inking the pigeon's lines it's time for you to create your Zendoodle art. Remember, start from wherever you wish to in your bird. Let your pen move freely through the bird's clearly defined body. Do not feel inhibited and certainly do not try to force anything to come forward. Letting your hand move of its own accord will allow you to create a stunning piece of Zendoodle art.

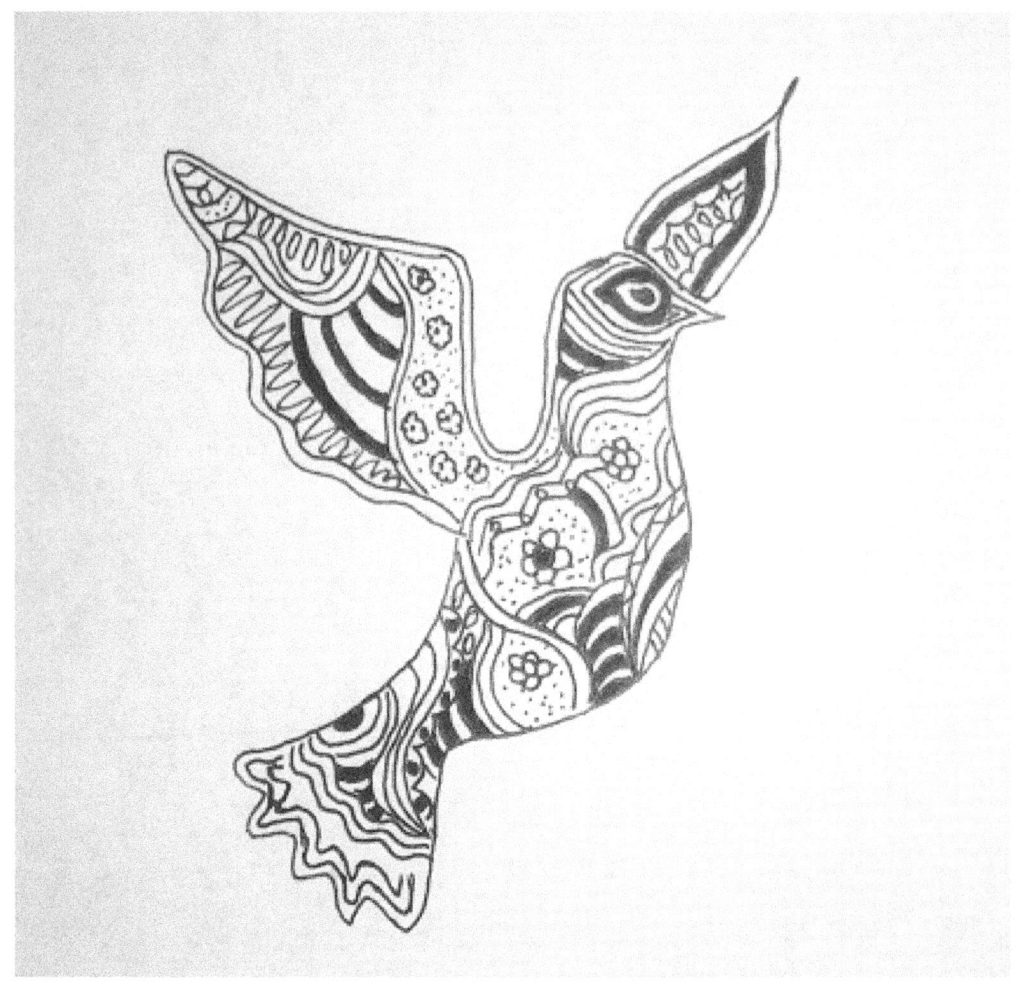

Congratulations! You have just completed the basic course in creating Zendoodle art. By drawing these three animals – the dolphin, the lizard, and the pigeon – as well as the three geometric shapes (square, circle and triangle), you have shown that you can master the basics of drawing. Having mastered these basics you moved on to the powerful, freeing art of a Zendoodle method.

Within the confines of the images you created you were able to bring something new and exciting to life. This is especially true in the pigeon which you just finished. While this image was of something as common as a pigeon, you turned it into something unique and uncommon. By letting your inner self guide your pen, by allowing it to creating Zendoodle art of stunning power and originality, you have made that pigeon come alive with a part of yourself.

Conclusion

Creating art is a beautiful and freeing experience. This holds true whether you are a metalsmith creating statues and free standing pieces, or a painter working with traditional oils. The simple fact concerning art is that it is a powerful experience. Not only is the artist moved through creating their piece but those who see the piece are moved as well.

This fact concerning art holds true for Zendoodle art as well. What's different about Zendoodle art, however, is the way that you allow your inner self to guide your hand. Not only is beautiful art created by your inner self but you have allowed yourself to relax in a deeper, more powerful fashion than traditional artwork would.

Your Zendoodle art is just that: yours. By using certain structures, such as the various animals and the basic shapes, you are allowing your creativity to explore the confines of a space which normally is not seen as a creative space. Who would think to use a pigeon to create powerful, flowing patterns? Who could have seen the beauty and the potential in something as simple as a triangle?

You must remember, as you practice your Zendoodle art and allow your inner self to flow out onto the page, that your potential is unlimited. Every blank page, every empty form and space is a place for you to relax and search yourself. Drawing your Zendoodle patterns will allow you to look within yourself, to find a quiet place in your mind so that each piece of Zendoodle art is not only a work of beauty but a powerful reminder that you have created an inner peace with each drawing.

Remember, Zendoodle art is nothing that should be forced or contrived. Each piece should be a reflection of your inner self as it moves across the page. Do not think and worry about the designs and patterns which you want to see within a specific shape that you have chosen, simply let those patterns flow. The fluidity and timelessness which you create with these patterns will be restful to your eye each time you look upon them. You will be able to remember that sense of peace that you felt as you created the Zendoodle art.

If you choose, as you finish each piece of Zendoodle art, you can add color to the patterns. If you do decide to do this do not forget that this act too should be reflective, an act which allows you to look within yourself as you lose yourself in the beauty of the art which you are creating.

www.ingramcontent.com/pod-product-compliance
Lightning Source LLC
Chambersburg PA
CBHW080605190526
45169CB00007B/2889